D1499961

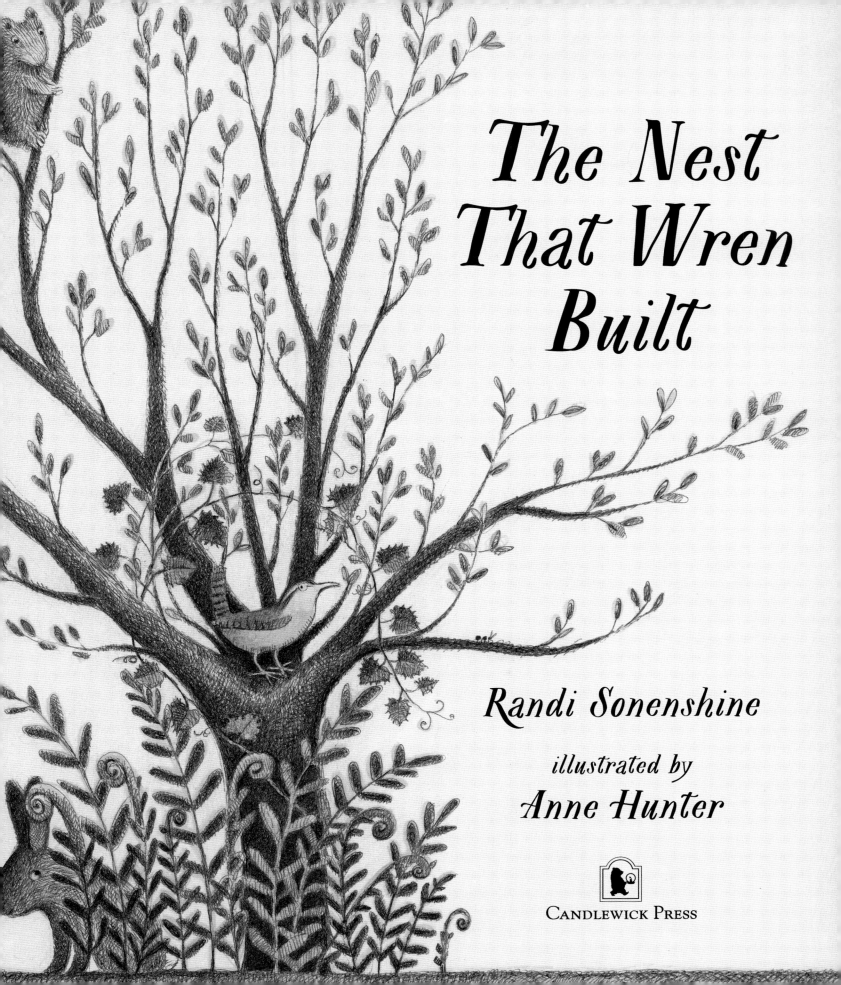

The Nest That Wren Built

Randi Sonenshine

illustrated by

Anne Hunter

CANDLEWICK PRESS

These are the twigs, dried in the sun,

that Papa collected one by one

to cradle the nest that Wren built.

This is the bark, snippets of twine,

spidery rootlets, and needles of pine

that shape the nest that Wren built.

These are the leaves of ruby and gold,

fallen from trees sturdy and old,

that weave through the nest that Wren built.

This is the sac, silky and white, brimming
with spiders who feast on the mites
that threaten the nest that Wren built.

This is the snakeskin warding off harm,
a scaly and thin reptilian charm,
draped on the nest that Wren built.

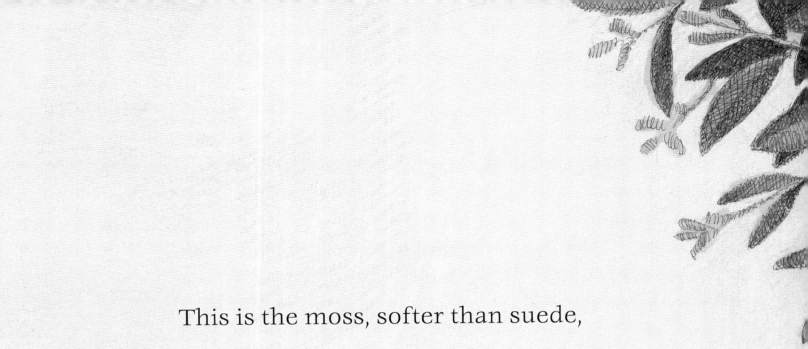

This is the moss, softer than suede,
stolen from stones cool in the shade
to line the nest that Wren built.

These are the feathers, petals, and thread
placed on the moss to soften the bed
that waits in the nest that Wren built.

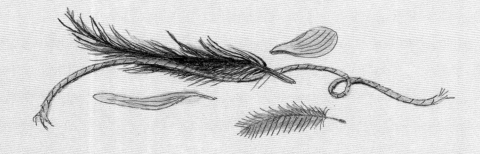

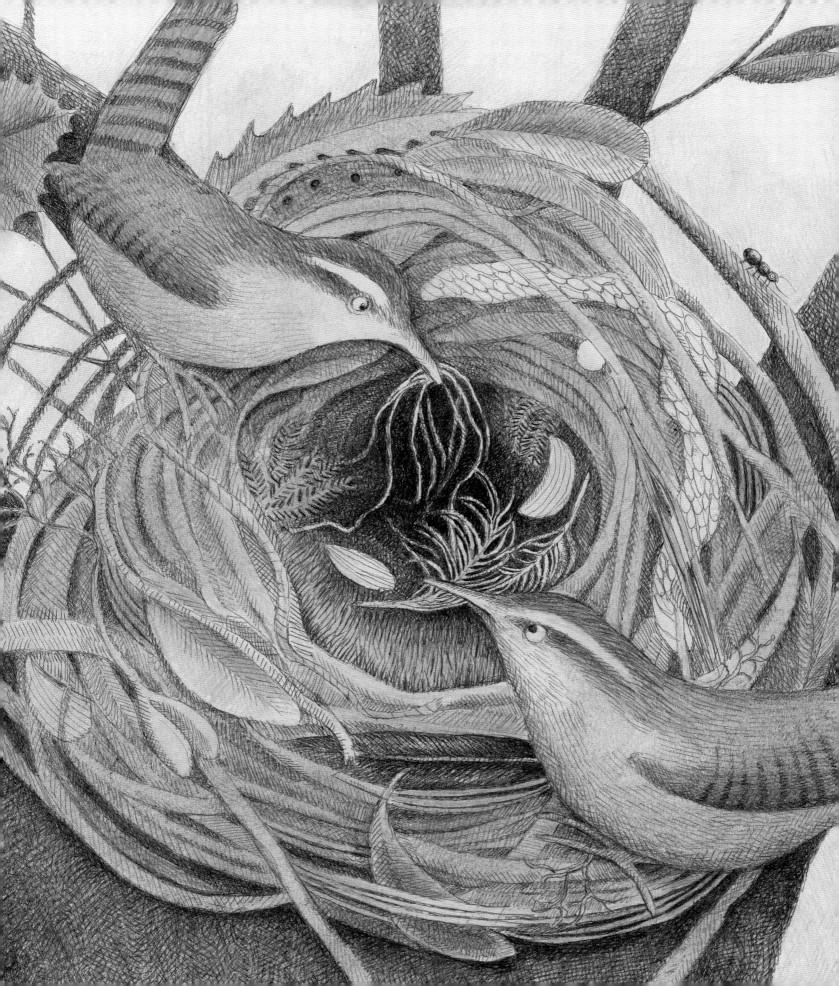

This is the tuft of rabbity fur,
plucked from a sharp, persnickety burr
to warm the nest that Wren built.

This is the papa perching nearby,
chirping a mirthful song to the sky
and guarding the nest that Wren built.

These are the eggs, laid on the bed
of velvety moss, feathers, and thread,
safe in the nest that Wren built.

These are the hatchlings scratching within,

stretching and pecking, all scrawny and thin,

that hatch in the nest that Wren built.

This is Papa hunting for food—
a spider or beetle to nourish the brood
that waits in the nest that Wren built.

These are the nestlings, drowsy and fed,
snuggly and plump on their feathery bed,
warm in the nest that Wren built.

These are the fledglings, fourteen days old.

They inch to the edge while feathers unfold . . .

then fly from the nest that Wren built.

Glossary

brood: a group of young birds that hatched at the same time

burr: a rough or prickly covering on a nut or seed

fledgling: a young bird that has just learned to fly

hatchling: a young bird that has just come out of an egg

mites: tiny insects that live and feed on plants and animals

nestling: a young bird that is not yet able to fly or leave the nest

nourish: to provide something with food and other things it needs to grow strong and healthy

reptilian: related to a reptile, which is a cold-blooded animal that lays eggs and is covered in scales or body armor, such as a snake, turtle, or alligator

rootlet: a small or thin branch of a root

spider sac: a silky cocoon containing a spider's eggs

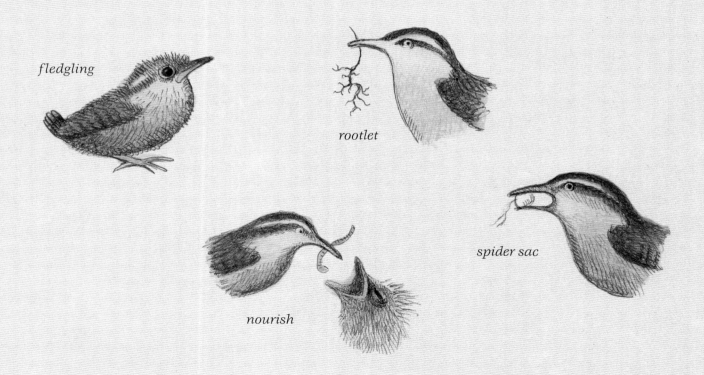

fledgling

rootlet

nourish

spider sac

Wren Facts

Location! Location! Location!

The male Carolina Wren builds up to a dozen "dummy" nests before singing a special song to attract a prospective mate. When a female wren answers the call, he takes her on a tour of his many starter homes.

A Real Stickler

Once a female wren approves of a starter nest, she may show her appreciation for her mate in a strange way: dismantling the nest and tossing out stick after stick while noisily scolding him! Both the male and the female take part in building the real nest, but the female is usually in charge of interior design; she constantly adds and rearranges the nesting material to create the perfect place to lay and incubate her eggs and care for her nestlings.

Built-in Pest Control

It's not unusual for Carolina Wrens to add spider sacs to their nesting materials. One theory is that when the baby spiders hatch, they eat mites, tiny parasites that infest the nest and can endanger the nestlings.

Sssss-strange Decorating

A snakeskin is often draped over the edge of a wren's nest like a piece of tinsel. But this shiny wall hanging is more than decoration. It's actually a clever trick to scare predators, especially flying squirrels, who love a good bird egg or two for breakfast!

Here, There, and Everywhere

Wrens are known for their odd choice of nesting sites. They are so well adapted to living around people that they will nest just about anywhere—near a house, even in a garage! It wouldn't be surprising to find a wren's nest inside a boot, a hanging flower basket, a watering can, or even a bike helmet!

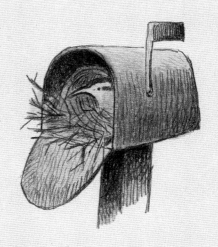

For my nestlings, Jake and Ethan,
and for Marty, who encouraged me to fly
R. S.

For the sake of wrens and ants
and quiet mossy places
A. H.

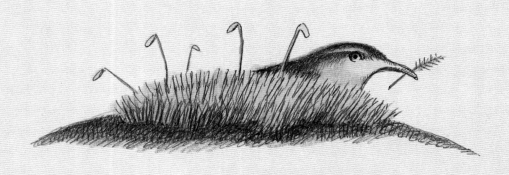

First edition 2020

Library of Congress Catalog Card Number 2020900502
ISBN 978-1-5362-0153-6

20 21 22 23 24 CCP 10 9 8 7 6 5 4 3 2

Printed in Shenzhen, Guangdong, China

This book was typeset in ITC Veljovic.
The illustrations were done in ink and colored pencil on tinted paper.

Candlewick Press
99 Dover Street
Somerville, Massachusetts 02144

visit us at www.candlewick.com